# The Library

# The Library

Patrick Carberry

**To order additional copies of this book, contact:**
Xlibris Corporation
1-888-795-4274
www.Xlibris.com
Orders@Xlibris.com
75860

# CONTENTS

# INTRODUCTION

This is a story of a man accused of a crime he did not commit. There are many innocent people in jail but because of a good judge who recognized a misinterpretation of actions and had a good understanding of individual character the correct decision was made. Much credit needs to be given to the defense attorney for her contribution and her ability to present the information on which the judge based his decision. It is important that nobody be offended as the story is told. This applies especially to the officer who was just doing his job, a job that many of us would not care to do.

It is my hope that you will agree with the judgment and you will conclude the same as the judge did and that you will enjoy the story. See what you think. It is my hope that you can take something positive from this story.

# CHAPTER ONE

## The Girl

The first time I ever saw this girl was outside the library. It was a warm day and I was standing in the sun enjoying it before starting my walk home. There were two girls hustling around the way girls do while waiting for a parent to pick them up after school. One girl went inside the library but one stayed outside. Looking over at her I smiled and she returned a smile with a little giggle. When she smiled it was obvious she had braces on her teeth. It was the only time I ever saw her smile. My heart immediately went out to her. She was a beautiful girl and someday the braces would be removed and her teeth would be beautiful just like the rest of her. She seemed so happy to be getting this attention and if she was enjoying it I was happy to provide it for her. No words were spoken and I began my walk home.

One day while sitting at a computer in the library I noticed this young girl to my left and slightly behind me. She was standing behind a display case and therefore was out of sight of the librarians. She had a camera/phone in her hand and was pointing it in my direction. She seemed more interested in whatever it was that was on the computer monitor than in me. Looking back at her I smiled. On this day it was the only day of my life that I had a camera. I was trying to send pictures to friend in California and we did not have use of the internet at home. In an attempt to play along with her I turned and took a snapshot of her. At some point I had moved to another computer not because she was disturbing me in any way but because it was my preference to use the computer facing the doors so I could see the people going in and out of the library. Once again this girl shows up behind me with camera in hand. Again she was behind bookcases and out of sight of the librarians. Moving my chair which was on wheels slightly to my right I turned toward her and took another snapshot. When leaving the library she was outside so I took one more picture. She had gone down to the next level in between some trees but she was sitting on a bench when I took the picture. I did not go down to the area where she was and the picture was taken from a distance.

I started to walk home. Almost home there seemed to be someone walking behind me. It was this young girl. Turning around and very surprised I said "Is there something I can do for you. She replied "No". She had removed the tongs or whatever you call the footwear she was wearing from her feet perhaps so that I would not hear her walking behind me.

When I turned toward her and began to speak she began to put her footwear back on. It seemed so dangerous that a young girl would follow an older man that she did not know and I had no clue why. Before the end of the day it became more clear that she was concerned about the pictures. Perhaps she had followed me so she could see where I lived so she could report it to the police. She asked "Can I take your picture?" In reply I said "sure". Again not understanding why it later became apparent she wanted the picture to take to the police. Living in this neighborhood for almost thirty years I had never seen this girl before except at the library. I asked "Do you live around here?" I did not ask her where she lived as she would later say. Although these two questions might sound the same there is an immense difference. The first question is very general and can be answered with a yes or no. The second question requires a more specific answer such as an address. She replied "I live back there" as she pointed over her shoulder. That could have been anywhere and I did not question her further. We began to walk down the street now only five houses from my house. She walked on the right side of the street and slightly ahead of me as I was on the left side of the street. When getting to the house I went around to the back door. It is unknown at this point whether she continued down the street or whether she turned back in the direction of the library. There was no attempt on my part to determine where she was going. It did seem rather dangerous that this girl was walking in a strange neighborhood.

# CHAPTER TWO

## Police

These pictures were taken on a Wednesday. On Wednesday my wife and I to to mass at 7pm. After mass we go out to eat. When we returned home it was probably after 9pm. And we had gone upstairs for the night. There was a knock at the door and the dog was barking. Going downstairs probably wearing very little, I then noticed a bright light shine in the front door. It alarmed me for a second and then I heard someone say police. Going to the door and opening it I stepped outside. There were two officers and one said "We would like to talk to you Mr. Carberry" I said "Is it ok if we talk out here not being aware that I was wearing very little. The officer said "It's kind of personal". So we stepped inside and I assured them that the dog would not harm them.

The officer began by saying "We understand that you were up at the library today and that there were pictures taken", and there was a complaint. I replied "Yes, I did. The officer then asked if he could see the camera. The camera was in the next room and I had it in his hand in less than a minute. He began looking at the pictures and then asked "Is this the girl?" I said "Yes". He then deleted the picture and the next two pictures. You would of thought that the pictures were of his own daughter. I told him I would of deleted the pictures myself but I didn't know how as it was not my camera. He showed me that by pressing the garbage can icon it was deleted. He then proc eded to look through the other pictures in the camera, probably about forty pictures. I guess he was looking to see if there were any other pictures of children. When he came to a picture of three young ladies he said "Who's that" I explained that it was my wife, her sister in law and her niece. Keep in mind that one lady was over sixty, one would be sixty in a few months and one was in her early twenties. I had no problem with him deleting the pictures or that matter looking at all the other pictures. It was not til much later that I realized he was doing this without a search warrant.

The officer then suggested that I avoid this young girl. It was my own suggestion that I could go to the library at a different time of day like in the morning while the girl was in school. Before the officers left I shook hands with both officers. Later that night I called the police station and talked to the officer. I asked him to tell the girl and the parents that the pictures were deleted from the camera and that there was no chance that the pictures would be on the internet. I also asked him to tell them that I was sorry. Whether or not he ever did this is not known. The officers were very professional and I appreciated that. I don't even remember seeing a police car in front of the house. However the lady next door did see the police and was questioning why.

# CHAPTER THREE

## Messages

The next day I was in the library when the girl comes in with a friend. They would go downstairs as I could see them from where I was sitting. She always looked my way but quickly looked away as they went down the steps. When they came back up they would sometimes go out in the lobby where there was a water fountain. You could see the wheels turning and I always knew what she was going to do. Before she would go home she would always make her way around the back of the library and she would come up behind me where she could see my computer monitor.

One day she came in earlier than usual and by herself Could she be skipping class or was going to the library part of the class. I overheard the librarian talking to her and she called her by name. So the next time she came up behind me I pulled up a screen so I could write her a message. It was actually my e-mail screen. I changed the font to the largest size so she would have no trouble reading it. The first day I wrote Hi _____. She always had a camera/phone or whatever this piece of technology was. She may have been using it to record these messages.

On the nest day the same thing happened She came in, went downstairs but before leaving she would come from behind me to look at what it was I was reading or the message I had written for her. On this day I wrote "You are soooo gorgeous. When God was giving out good looks you must of gotten in line twice". This time it was her friend who had the camera and was recording the message. It was the only time her friend ever came around.

On the third day and the final day the same thing happened. The message was "You are going to need a baseball bat to keep all the boys away". But on this day one of the librarians noticed her behind me. The librarians then huddled. Seeing this I got up and left the library because I did not want her to get in trouble. Whether or not she ever got in trouble is not known. It was the last time I would see her as I guess the school year was over.

# CHAPTER FOUR

## Police Again

One day as I was walking the dog I came to the community church, parking lot and community center. Along side the parking lot is a grassy area with a picnic table. I sat down for a moment and I noticed a police car in the parking lot on the other side of the lot. I thought the officer was watching for car speeding. Then I saw another police car go by. The policeman who was parked in the parking lot drove over to me. He said "Mr. Carberry, did you get the citation I sent you?" I replied "No, citation for what?" He said "You are being charged with harassment". He then started to read the messages I had written which were on his computer in the police car. Harassment I said, I have not ever seen this person. It had been six days since the last time I had seen her. It was apparent to me that the girl had recorded these messages because when the officer was reading them to me they were exactly what I had written.

I tried to explain my profile as a former elementary teacher, a nurse for over twenty years and a member of the community for almost thirty years. He seemed interested in the part about being an elementary teacher. He said he had to go and drove off.

Later that day I went down to the police station to talk to the officer. It was my belief that nothing good could come of going to court with this. Not for the girl, not for the officer and certainly not for me. We again talked about my backround. He was not impressed and he said "the toothpaste is already out of the tube". He said that the case was now in the hands of the court and once it is in the hands of the court there is nothing they can do about it. He asked me why I took the pictures and I said "she had a camera and I had a camera". He called me a liar. Our conversation soon ended as we both left the room and he went to the back and I went home. I was very concerned about my reputation if people would hear about this.

One morning I was walking home from church as I do almost every morning in the summer when I noticed a police car stopped at a stop sign. I hurried over to the police car. There were two police officers in the car both were elderly gentlemen. I said "I like to make an appointment to talk to the Chief of Police if that is possible. The officer in the driver seat said "When do you want to come in ?" I said "Whenever it is convenient for him" The officer in the passenger seat was the Chief of Police" which I did not know at the time. He said, "How about 10am?". I said, "good" "Who should I ask for?" I answered my own question. The Chief of Police. He just nodded affirmatively. I said thanks and continued to walk home. It was just after 8am so I had some time to do some things around the house before I began to walk down to the police station. I got there early and the lady in the office told me to have a seat after telling her that I had an appointment at 10am to see the Chief of Police. It seemed like a long time but, it was only minutes before he came out and we went back to the conference room for our discussion. It was the same room where I had spoken with the accusing officer. I was asking for his advise as I told him the story. He listened attentively, the topics we discussed will be mentioned later in an effort not to repeat myself. His advice wa to show up for the hearing at the assigned time and date and to be on time. I already knew this but I could appreciate what he was telling me. He also told me that I could have an attorney accompany me. This was good advice and I remembered a friend who was an attorney. He told me that the case was in the hands of the district magistrate and that there was nothing they could do. This was what the officer presenting the citation had told me also. When we were finished talking we both got up and walked out of the room as I thanked him for his time and wished him a good day. He replied "You do the same" I began my walk home.

# CHAPTER FIVE

## A Day in Court

It was over a month before the hearing so and I kept hoping I had the right day because if you don't show up for the hearing you get arrested. One day I met with my attorney. She was a wonderful lady and very good at law proceedings. We talked about what had happened and she felt strongly as I did that no crime had been committed. She later did some research on the specific charge which was harassment.

The day of the hearing was rainy day and I had accidentally left the window in my van down overnight. The driver seat was wet when I was going to church that morning. Not a good way to start the day. There was a plastic cover which had been used to cover the seat when the vehicle was being inspected. It worked well and kept my clothes from getting wet.

Dressed in my suit I arrived early. I was getting a little nervous after waiting over an hour because my attorney had not arrived yet. I went into the building and to the window of the office and asked on of the ladies what time it was. They looked at me like I was some kind of a criminal but said it was two thirty. The hearing was scheduled for three fifteen. At some point while waiting for my attorney to arrive I had gone into the building and noticed the judge. He came out of the courtroom and was talking to a young man about some unpaid fines. I could tell just by the way he was talking to this young person that he was a fair man. I felt better already. Outside my attorney had arrived shortly after. As we were talking I noticed the young girl and her family going into the building. I wasn't even sure it was her. We went into the building but we were seated in an area that was separated from the area where the girl was sitting. We were totally out of each other's view.

After a while the police officer came in and I said "Hi". He replied "Hi" abruptly. My attorney immediately knew what type of an individual he was. All the other policemen I had seen that day were friendly. He went into the courtroom and came back out and started to direct the girl and her family into the courtroom. My attorney and I followed. We sat on the left side of the room and the officer, the girl and her family sat on the right. We all took the oath to tell the truth the whole truth and nothing but the truth. I wasn't looking at anyone else but just assumed that everyone would tell the truth. When the hearing started I realized that I had made a false assumption.

The officer started the proceedings telling the district magistrate what I had done. He stated that I had taken pictures of the girl without her permission. As the officer was asking the girl questions it occurred to me that more and more of what was being said was not entirely truthful. How could this be after all we had all just taken an oath to tell the truth. For example, the girl was trying to convince the court that she did not follow me home after the pictures were taken. She was walking behind me going in the opposite direction of the library and possibly her house. She started by saying that she waited 15 minutes after I had left the library. This was totally untrue. It is improper to speak out in court and any response was to be made by the attorney and not me. After hearing this it was necessary to say something. The defense attorney said go ahead. The judge permitted me to speak and I said, "Your honor, I go to the library every day and it takes me less than 10 minutes to go to or from. To say she waited 15 minutes after I left is not even possible and I would of already been home. She was off to a bad start in her effort to convince the court that she did not follow me home.

The judge listened closely and took notes the whole time. Later when the defense attorney was questioning the girl about her following me home the officer shouted out "objection". Again it would have been out of place for me to interrupt but if I could I would of objected to his objection. First of all, as the good judge said the officer does not know what happened because he was not there. Any information he does have is second hand at very best. I on the other hand was there and have an almost vivid memory of what happened.

If I could of spoken I would of told the officer that I could calculate the number of steps behind me she was but that he and the members of the court would probably agree that was not necessary. The young girl said about twenty feet and that was acceptable. Second of all we all have to keep in mind that we are listening to the testimony of a young girl. She has my admiration because at that age I don't know if I could of done what she was doing (testifying in a court of law). The third thing we as members of the court have to keep in mind is that we took an oath to tell the truth. There seemed to be some untruthful statements made even if not on purpose. It is important to remember that the judge has a decision to make and the least we can do is to allow him to make this decision based on truth and not some fabricated story. It is the most important decision of my life. Let's put the truth right on the table.

When she was following me I turned around and she was right there. I spoke to her. Now I would not be speaking to her if she was three blocks away. I said to her in a polite voice, "Is there something I can do for you?". She replied "No". I was concerned for her to say the least.

She had at some point told the members of the court that I asked her where she live. I did not. I asked her if she lived on this street which is the street that I had lived on for almost thirty years. She replied "No I live back there".

When my attorney questioned the officer about the fact that he looked at pictures in the camera without a search warrant, he turned away from us and said, "This is not about the pictures. Well lets agree with him for a moment, after all the pictures were deleted within hours after taken. It was like they never existed. But the officer had written on the citation that pictures were taken without permission. I had the citation with me in court. The officer also asked me why I took the pictures when I went to the police station to talk to him. He called me a liar after I had just given him what I thought was a pretty honest answer. Seems to me like he is shooting himself in the foot. Oouch! But when he was looking at the pictures in the camera which had nothing to do with this case he was invading my privacy. There was a picture of my wife in her robe after she had just awakened which I can guarantee she would not of wanted him to see. So now he was not only invading my privacy but he was invading hers also. He was doing this without a search warrant. Who is breaking the law now officer?

The officer also stated that he was invited into the home. "Red flag". Criminals do not invite police officers into their home. "Red flag" Criminals do not come down to the police station to talk to the officer about charges against them. "Red flag" Criminals do not make an appointment to talk to the Chief of Police". What was it about this officer that was causing him to miss all these red flags. This was not someone who had just moved into the neighborhood or from somewhere else for that matter. This was a man who lived in the community for almost thirty years. This was not someone with a criminal record but, someone who had never been in trouble in his whole life. This was not some kind of a delinquent or high school dropout but, a man with three college degrees. He had worked for over thirty years which included positions in elementary education and over twenty years of nursing. This was a guy who walked to church daily and most recently had even attended church twice a day and on rare occasion three time a day. It just does not sound like the profile of a criminal especially when you consider that I have not done anything illegal.

When I spoke to the Chief of Police, he told me that they did not have a profile of an individual until they presented themselves. But the officer has a computer in his police car and had access to all this information and even after it was presented in court it was like he could not process it. It was like a college professor once told me that I could not see the forest through the trees. It seems fishy to me, and was this officer somehow related to this young girl or even just a neighbor.

Here we have an officer coming to my house and going through pictures without a search warrant and a young girl coming up behind me in the library and looking at and possibly recording information from the computer that I was using. Maybe I was the one who was being harassed.

The officer at some point asked why I left teaching. He was insinuating that I had some problem with the children. I started to tell him that when I graduated from college I took a job in the hospital for the summer. He then said "You got another job" and seemed satisfied with that answer. But, if he would of allowed me to continue I would of told him that in the fall I began substitute teaching in the same school district. In that school district you had to choose an area to teach. I selected grades four throughsix. Teacher from other grades would tell me that they wanted me to substitute for them but for example an eighth grade teacher, but that I was committed to grades four through six. It was a great compliment to me that I was the one that they wanted to be with their kids. So he really missed the boat when he tried to find some dirt on me in the teaching profession.

In the 90's I had a swimming pool in my back yard. People would allow their children to come to swim but no adults ever came to supervise them. Not only did they trust me around their children but they trusted me with their lives because of the risk with water safety.

So now we get to the previously mentioned messages which were on the computer which the young girl would read and possibly record with her camera. The messages were very complimentary. There was never anything derogatory, never anything offensive and certainly never anything that could be considered harassing. These messages were not sent to the girls home and the only way she could even read them was by coming up behind me while I was at the computer. The officer had stated that the girl had the messages on her computer at home. If I was a young girl and somebody thought that I was gorgeous you bet I would have them on my computer too. I would probably print it out and save it for life.

The officer picked up the camera that was sitting on the table to show me that the camera/phone could be used to send text messages and had other functions. So what was he saying, that the girl had not recorded the messages. He just got done saying that she had the messages on her computer at home, so how did the messages get from the library computer to her home computer if she was not in some way recording them. Did he shoot himself in the foot again? Double oouch.

I looked at the camera/phone on the table and said to the officer; "Is that the phone she had?" He said, "I guess so". What kind of a reply is that. He had taken an oath to tell the truth and now he is saying "I guess so". Well in fact the phone/camera she had at the library was white or some shade of white but, the one on the table was black. This is not of major importance and I didn't say anything but it does make one wonder about the accuracy and the validity of the testimony presented.

If the glove does not fit you must acquit. Well that might of not been true in OJ Simpsons case but it was true this time. If only I were allowed to speak Johnny Cochran would be rolling on the floor laughing because I'd be dancing.

Now let us turn our attention to the charge of harassment. Harassment refers to a wide spectrum offensive behaviors. The term commonly refers to behavior intended to disturb or upset and when the term is used in the legal text it refers to behavior which are found to be threatening or disturbing. Sexual harassment refers to persistent unwanted sexual advances. If someone told you that you were gorgeous would you consider that to be threatening or disturbing and if you did consider it disturbing would you come back the next day for more?

Never was there anything considered to be offensive nor was there any intent to be offensive. Never was there anything meant to disturb or upset and certainly nothing considered to be threatening. It was all complimentary and if I were a young girl and someone told me I was gorgeous, I would smile say thank you and keep on walking. If anything was found to be offensive by anyone then they are severely misinterpreting the statement.

I want to know who thinks that this is harassment. If it is the young girl, why would she go out of her way to make her way around the back of the library and come up behind me to read these messages, not once but on three consecutive days. To be harassed? Not likely. If it were a parent who thought that the girl was being harssed then why would they not tell their girl to stay away from this man. And finally was this something fabricated by the officer to make me stay away from the girl after complete separation had already been achieved. After all I had not even seen the girl since school was over not to mention the fact that at no point did I ever approach this girl. The citation was dated June 16, and the last time I had seen the girl was June 10.

When the judge gave the mother of the girl her chance to speak, she said that the girl was afraid to go out of the house. Imagine that, the girl was not afraid when she followed me home. The girl was not afraid when on three separate occasions she came up behind me to read the messages. But the most convincing of all is the fact that when asked by the judge if she was afraid of this man she replied under oath "No, not physically". There might be a good explanation why she was not afraid and that might be that I never gave her any reason to be afraid.

When she followed me home it seemed so dangerous for a young girl to follow a man she does not know but in retrospect if I could pick any man in the world for her to follow home, she picked the right man because this man was no more of a threat to her than Mr. Rogers would be. I would not hurt this girl for all the rice in China.

When the girl was being questioned by the officer she stated that at one point I had thrown her a kiss. This might have been only the second time I ever saw her and it was while she was standing behind the display case with the camera pointed at me. She immediately ran down the steps I guess to tell her girlfriend. I was happy if she was excited about that.

Another thing she said was that I had made a heart out of the cord of my earphones. I thought this was so cute but I had no idea it even happened. When using earphones there is a wire that comes down on both sides of the face and comes together at about chest level, very much like the shape of a heart. What imagination, I gave her an A+ for originallity. I must have been smiling from ear to ear when I heard this in court.

When the judge gave the father of the girl a chance to speak he stated that for a man this age to be interacting with a young girl was disgusting. These were not his exact words except for disgusting but you get the idea. I wonder what it was that was so disgusting. Was it telling the girl that she was gorgeous? Imagine if it would have been something offensive. Ok, I would agree with him if this were a child predator. If this were my child and a child predator came near her I would want to dismember him with my own hands. But this was not a child predator or any other type of criminal. This was a man who lived in the community for almost thirty years and was never in his life in any type of trouble. With this type of reputation I might smile knowing someone thought she was gorgeous because not only was this a compliment to the girl but it is also a compliment to the mother and father.

We as a society have become so brain washed because if a criminal act is committed it is so publicized, it makes us all aware of the occurrence. It is on the news, on TV, on radio, on the internet, in the newspaper ect. On the other hand when a good deed is done nobody knows about it.

Here is the part of the story that is so difficult to understand. Why was the officer and the parents unable to see the facts and the red flags that this was not a criminal. What was it that was motivation for the officer to send this man to jail.

Was he somehow involved. The parents did not know me and probably never saw me before even though they may attend the same church as me. But the officer seemed to have some special interest in this case. Was he a neighbor or was he a relative such as an uncle to this young girl. Someone suggested the possibility that there was money involved. I doubt it after all wouldn't that be bribing a police officer. Perhaps it was just pride. Now our community seems to have very little crime although the police department might dispute this, and this would be a major event to send someone to jail. But, how would a police officer or the young girl or the parents sleep at night if they knew they were responsible for sending an innocent man to jail. Our jails are overcrowded enough and if this happened it may even cause a good man to turn bad. Just what our society needs right?

Finally I get my chance to speak in court, but the judge wanted me to limit my time to the events of May 6 and May 9. My attorney introduced me by telling the members of the court that it is not normal procedure to allow the defendant to speak but, this man was the most honest and considerate person that she had ever known. I will always remember and appreciate that from her.

Well I tried to limit my discussion but I told the judge that the area I was most interested in addressing was the idea of harassment. He agreed to that. I would try to tell my story more correctly than some of the other members of the court had done as honesty is so important to me.

First of all if this were harassment why would this young girl go out of her way to go around the back of the library and come up behind me to read these messages or anything else for that matter. She was able to disguise it very well because there were bookcases behind me which shielded her from the view of the librarians and even if they could see her she was able to make it look like she was looking at a book. Does this sound like somebody being harassed. After all she was doing this on her own and there was nobody trying to influence her or persuade her to do so. If this were harassment she had many other things she could be doing.

Second of all if this were harassment why would I not of brought this to the attention of the librarians?

Thirdly and maybe most important of all, why when the librarian noticed the girl overlooking my computer would I get up and leave the library for the specific reason that I did not want her to get in trouble. If this were harassment I would of stayed and made sure she got in trouble. I kept my story short as promised as we had already been in court over two hours and the judge had sent his staff home. He was a patient man.

The judge now asked the girl if she was afraid of this man. She replied "No, not physically" This was all he needed to know if he was not already convinced that this man was not guilty. The judge looked directly at the mother of the girl and stated "I know you would like to see this man go to jail but I find him not guilty" You see fear is an important component of harassment. The judge explained this to the parents of the girl and told them how he had kept notes all during the case as he held up his notebook and flipped through the pages.

The judge also stated that he would keep the case open for 120 days This could be used to convince anyone who had any doubt because if this man was any type of a threat to the girl it would surface very quickly and would of surfaced long before this. This also provided a chance for people to pursue the case and to try to obtain evidence which would convince guilt of the individual.

The judge then spoke to the young girl and said "If you see this man I want you to go to the other side of the street. The judge never even looked in my direction but I knew that I was to avoid this young girl.

The mother of the girl was not pleased but it was understood that this was a warning but the mother felt that there already was a warning. Not true. When the officers came to my house it was like a suggestion that I avoid this girl. They did not say anything to the effect that if I did not, then this another set of events would occur such as some type of reprimand or even jail time. But when the officer was in court he stated that I had been warned under nouncertain terms. Not true. But I did avoid going to the library at that time of the day while the girl might be there. That did not last very long.

When I spoke with the Chief of Police one of the things we discussed was going to the library at this time of the day. I said "For me not to go to the library between 2;30pm and 4pm would be like telling the girl that she could not go during that time period. This would be a disservice to her and if this was where her parents were picking her up after school it would be a disservice to them. The Chief responded, "We would not tell you or anyone else that they could not go to the library at any time of day, it is a public place and it is anyone's right to go ". In response to the mother saying I was warned to stay away not only was I not warned but, I was well within my rights to go there at that time. However after we went to court and during the 120 day period I did avoid going at that time and I even went to other libraries which were much further away from my home.

As the girl and her family and the officer left the courtroom I approached the bench because I wanted to ask the judge if after the 120 days I was found not guilty would my fee be refunded. Normally I would of asked one of the staff members but they had already gone home for the day. He gave me an affirmative answer and he asked that I say a prayer for him. Little did he know that I had been praying for him, the girl and the officer for weeks. When I approached the bench my attorney immediately told me that if was not proper to approach the judge at this time. The reason the judge asked for a prayer was because during the proceedings my attorney had questioned me about the various churches I attended and there locations and even the names of the priest. I knew all those answers well. The was very interested especially in the locations and I think he may have been Roman Catholic also.

The judge had also suggested to my attorney before we left the courtroom that she read the words written by a famous attorney which was displayed outside the courtroom. He was an attorney himself for over forty years.

Outside the courtroom while my attorney was trying to copy the words on display as the judge had suggested that she read, I noticed outside the building but just out of the rain the girl, her family and the officer were talking. After a short while they dispersed. It was now time to lock up the building as the judge came out but he noticed the attorney reading the display and told her to take her time. I was right beside her when I heard the judge saying how he was a soccer coach, and had placed a hand on the shoulder of one of the children and was told by his wife who was an elementary teacher that this might be considered inappropriate. So he knew that someone had misinterpreted my actions.

After talking for a few minutes out in the rain my attorney and I went home.

# CHAPTER SIX

## 120 days

It was more than 120 days but it seemed like forever and the hearing was postponed for one week which made it seven days longer. The reason it seemed so long because the fine paid was more than $300.00 and I was expecting to have that refunded if I was not guilty.

One day while in church it hit me like a bolt of lightning it occurred to me that the reason the judge had only given me a short period of time to speak was because he had already been convinced of my innocence. He knew from my lifestyle of going to church on a daily basis and my previous history of never being in trouble that this was not a criminal. Add to that the fact that at least in my own mind that I had not done anything wrong.

On Friday Aug 7, at approximately 3;20pm this young girl and a tall lady with blond hair came into the library while I was working on this story. I wanted to get up and leave immediately but if I did I would lose all the work already done which was over ten pages. The two individuals went downstairs just like the girl would do when she came in with her friend. It occurred to me that perhaps the parents had some type of escort to keep the girl out of trouble. By the time I was able to get my story filed away they had come back upstairs. They were standing less than twenty feet from me. As I was leaving I had to walk behind them. I left without even looking in their direction. As I was walking up the street I noticed a police car coming down the street but instead of turning right he past the library and made the next left. Later that day I was talking to my attorney and telling her about the girl and the lady who was with her. As previously mentioned I had thought this lady was someone to provide some guidance for the girl but when speaking to the attorney she had other ideas. She started screaming at me over the phone that this was some type of trap and that the lady with the girl was a witness. The fact that I did not leave immediately was a bad start to the 120 days continuation. She cautioned me to stay away from that library and to use another library or at least to change my schedule so that I was not there when the girl was. So from that point on I never went to the library between 2;30pm and 4pm. I started to use other libraries which was inconvenient for me because this library was only minutes away for me.

On August 27 there was a police car parked across the street from my house. The lady who lived in that house worked as a cross guard and was considered as a member of the police4 department. So it was not unusual for a police car to stop by. All these event involving a police car happened after 3pm which was the shift the accusing officer worked.

On August 29, at approximately 5pm when my wife was leaving for church and I was taking the dog for a walk we both noticed this police car parked approximately 1000 feet from the house. When he saw both of us leaving he pulled away.

This officer has the right to observe me but my question is Doesn't he have anything better to do? Isn't there some dirt bag that is a threat to society that he could be observing rather than some innocent man.

There were other instances of strange behavior but because of my poor vision I could never identify who it was driving the police car. But why would any other officer behave this way?

The police in this community have been wonderful and for the most part still are. I wave whenever a police car passes and they sometimes wave back and even toot the horn.

On the day before the hearing I was walking the dog and I noticed a young girl walking in the area but she was far enough away that I could not distinguish if it was this same girl, but I was not going to get close enough to find out. I started to walk in the opposite direction and I noticed three or four girls walking toward me. I continued walking with the dog around the church. At some point I noticed this same girl coming up the street that I was approaching. I stopped and turned to go a different way and there behind me were these same three or four girls. Was this some type of trap, was there an unmarked car watching us. If this was a trap it was avoided well and if anyone was not convinced that there was nothing going on between me and the girl they should definitely be convinced now.

# CHAPTER SEVEN

## The End

December 9, finally came. The weather forecast included a winter storm. I had not used my vehicle for a while and I wondered if it would even start. If it started would it make it up the driveway because of the ice. The weather was mild and only slightly wet.

The hearing was for 9:30 am but I was out of bed at 8am. I had a medical emergency the night before but I was fine by morning. Arriving at the District Magistrate Court by 8:30am I was the only one there. When I went to sign in I noticed the judge and he must of noticed me as he was talking to a member of his staff. I stood out like a sore thumb because I was dressed in my suit and the other people who later came in wore jeans and sweatshirts and torn clothing.

People started to truck in, including the girl and her mother and a small child. It was unusual to see a child there. You would think that since my hearing was originally scheduled a week ago that I would be first. Think again. When the judge called me back it was only me and the girl and her family. The judge came to the office window and looked at me and said, "Sir, you have been here a long time come on back. My attorney did not arrive and I later found out that she was ill. The officer was not there either. Proceeding to enter the courtroom it was just me and the judge and an officer but not the officer associated with this case. Before I could even sit down the judge said "Sir, your case has been dismissed". It would have been easy to turn around and walk out of the courtroom but I knew that the girl and her mother were out in the waiting room. I told the judge that the girl and her mother were out in the waiting room and he asked me to tell them to come back. He then realized that this might be uncomfortable for me. The officer who was sitting in the courtroom then volunteered to ask them to come back. When they came in and sat down the judge then asked if there had been any other problems. The mother replied "No". The judge then tried to explain that this was a misunderstanding. He also told the story of how as a soccer coach for young children he was told by his wife (an elementary teacher) that placing his hand on a child's shoulder could be considered inappropriate. He then said to the mother that he didn't think there would be any more problems with Mr. Carberry. I then asked the judge if the fined I had paid would be refunded and he replied, "Yes" I don't remember if I thanked him or not and if I did he may of not heard me. After waiting while the girl and her mother left I then went home.

The next day my attorney informed me by e-mail that she was unable to attend the hearing because of an illness and that she was glad the case was dismissed.

# CHAPTER EIGHT

## Questions

Why was this young girl so interested in what was on the computer screen in front of me. Was she trying to record something, was she working on some type of project for school. Is there any other person in the world that she would approach this way. Surely the fact that she was standing behind the display case so the librarians could not see her meant that she was taking a chance. The librarians would never tolerate someone possibly copying the contents of another persons private matters. Usually I would read the newspaper online, get my e-mail and listen to music from the sixties. None of these things would be of interest to her. Was this just her idea of a game that went wrong when I pulled out a camera of my own. Maybe it was that I was so tolerent that I was easy prey. The answer to this question may never be known and only the girl would know.

When she had her picture taken what was a game now turned to a serious matter. It was ok when she was the one with the camera but now someone had turned the table on her and you would of thought the world was coming to an end. What if this man put her picture on the internet. So this was why she followed me home and took my picture so she could take it to the police. Now she not only had my picture to tell the police who was taking her picture at the library but she also knew the address.

Why me? She certainly did not have any interest in me, a man old enough to be her grandfather.

Did she really want to see me go to jail or was she just trying to please an adult such as her parents or the officer.

Why was the officer so irritated with me. Was he somehow related to the girl or just a neighbor or friend. What would he have to gain by seeing me go to jail? Was it money, pride or something else or all the above. When this officer came to my house to inquire about pictures that were taken he deleted the pictures from the camera so fast you would of thought the pictures were of his own daughter.

As much as I would like to know the answers to some of these questions, it is expected to never happen.

# CHAPTER NINE

## Lessons learned

When meeting with the accusing officer it was my feeling that nothing good could come of taking this matter to court. Not for him, not for the girl and certainly not for me. I was wrong. I began going to church more often, saying more prayers and giving more contributions to the church and related causes.

Even after the hearing in July I continued to pray for the girl, her parents, the officer, the judge, my attorney and especially for me. This can be considered a good thing. It seems like now that I have been found not guilty several months later that I continue to pray for all the characters involved.

It should be noted that we can all learn from this that one must make a judgment based on facts and not unknowns. We as a society can benefit from a story like this. Most people are good but it is always the bad that stand out and are greatly publicized. Good deeds go unnoticed. We need to understand that a good person can be misinterpreted and need to caution against prejudice. Not every man that walks down the street is a child predator.

On two occasions I said I was sorry but never did I feel that I had done anything wrong. After all I went through nobody ever told me that they were sorry even though it was not me misinterpreting another actions.

Maybe this was a small cross for me to carry from the good Lord and if so I accept it with a smile. I wish the best to the girl, her family, the officer and everybody involved. May God bless you and brighten your day.

www.ingramcontent.com/pod-product-compliance
Lightning Source LLC
Chambersburg PA
CBHW050345290526
45785CB00006B/2643